RACE IN
AMERICA

RACE AND POLICING

BY DUCHESS HARRIS, JD, PHD,
AND REBECCA RISSMAN

CONTENT CONSULTANT
Mark A. Edwards
Professor of Law
Mitchell Hamline School of Law

Essential Library

An Imprint of Abdo Publishing | abdopublishing.com

ABDOPUBLISHING.COM

Published by Abdo Publishing, a division of ABDO, PO Box 398166, Minneapolis, Minnesota 55439. Copyright © 2018 by Abdo Consulting Group, Inc. International copyrights reserved in all countries. No part of this book may be reproduced in any form without written permission from the publisher. Essential Library™ is a trademark and logo of Abdo Publishing.

Printed in the United States of America, North Mankato, Minnesota
042017
092017

 THIS BOOK CONTAINS RECYCLED MATERIALS

Interior Photos: Shutterstock Images, 4–5, 53; New York Daily News/Getty Images, 7; John Minchillo/AP Images, 12; Morphart Creation/Shutterstock Images, 14–15; Bettmann/Getty Images, 19; Horace Cort/AP Images, 26–27; AP Images, 30, 32, 49; Scott Applewhite/AP Images, 35; Peter Morgan/AP Images, 40–41; Alex Milan Tracy/Sipa USA/Newscom, 44; Seth Wenig/AP Images, 56–57; Michael Matthews/Police Images/Alamy, 63; Andy Katz/Pacific Press/LightRocket/Getty Images, 64–65; Michael Nigro/Pacific Press/Alamy, 69; Michael B. Thomas/AFP/Getty Images, 72; Joseph Sohm/Visions of America LLC/Alamy, 74–75; Noah Berger/AP Images, 78; Jim Mone/AP Images, 82–83; Max Becherer/AP Images, 84; Andrew Lichtenstein/Corbis News/Getty Images, 86–87; Mary Altaffer/AP Images, 89; Arne Dedert/picture-alliance/dpa/AP Images, 97

Editor: Nick Rebman
Series Designer: Maggie Villaume

PUBLISHER'S CATALOGING-IN-PUBLICATION DATA

Names: Harris, Duchess, ; Rissman, Rebecca, authors.
Title: Race and policing / by Duchess Harris, JD, PhD and Rebecca Rissman.
Description: Minneapolis, MN : Abdo Publishing, 2018. | Series: Race in America |
    Includes bibliographical references and index.
Identifiers: LCCN 2016962259 | ISBN 9781532110351 (lib. bdg.) |
    ISBN 9781680788204 (ebook)
Subjects: LCSH: Race--Juvenile literature. | Racial profiling in law enforcement--
    Juvenile literature. | Racism--Juvenile literature.
Classification: DDC 363.2--dc23
LC record available at http://lccn.loc.gov/2016962259

CONTENTS

"I CAN'T BREATHE"

July 17, 2014, was a hot, sunny afternoon on Staten Island, New York. Two police officers cruised the streets in an unmarked police car. Soon, they saw a familiar face. Eric Garner, an African American man, stood outside a beauty supply store.

Garner was a popular member of his community. People around the neighborhood called him Big E. The nickname was a good fit. Garner stood six feet two inches (188 cm) tall and weighed nearly 400 pounds (180 kg). Garner was known for being a peacemaker and a friendly presence in the area. Earlier that day, he had helped break up a neighborhood fight. When two men had begun to scuffle, Garner held the men apart. "You can't keep doing this," Garner had said. "There are kids out here."[1]

The police saw Garner in a different light. He often sold illegal goods on the street, such as individual cigarettes known as loosies. He had already been arrested twice in 2014 for this crime.

Two plainclothes police officers got out of their unmarked car. One officer, Justin Damico, approached Garner. The other, Daniel Pantaleo, stood nearby. The situation quickly escalated.

"Every time you see me, you want to mess with me," Garner said. "I'm tired of it," he continued. "It stops today. . . . I'm minding my business, officer. I'm minding my business. Please just leave me alone. I told you the last time, please just leave me alone."[2]

Garner resisted as the two officers tried to grab his hands. Officer Pantaleo grabbed Garner from behind and held him in a choke hold. A group of other officers soon arrived on the scene. The other officers assisted as Pantaleo brought Garner down onto the ground. Pantaleo then pressed Garner's face into the sidewalk while more officers moved in. Together, the police restrained Garner

Officer Pantaleo applies a choke hold on Garner while other officers arrive.

by pressing his chest and holding him down. Garner was handcuffed, and he repeated the phrase "I can't breathe" over and over.[3]

Police supervisors arrived on the scene. "Let up," one of them advised the group. "You got him already."[4] In the confusion of the scene, the officers holding Garner down may not have heard these commands. They continued to hold him down. Garner lost consciousness.

A swarm of pedestrians and law enforcement officials watched as paramedics arrived on the scene. They felt for Garner's pulse and urged him to wake up. When he failed to regain consciousness, paramedics put him into an ambulance and drove him to a nearby hospital. Approximately one hour later, Garner was pronounced dead.

At first, it looked as if Garner had died as a result of health problems. The 43-year-old father of six was in poor health. He was obese. He had heart disease. And he had asthma, a condition that can make breathing difficult. No one at the hospital believed Garner's death was related to the way the police had treated him.

After Garner died, police officers immediately made an official report of his arrest. In it, several officers said they did not think Garner was in danger.

Officers Pantaleo and Damico were young but experienced. Damico had been on the force since 2010. Pantaleo had joined in 2006 and usually focused on violent street crime. Pantaleo had a mixed reputation. He had achieved a good record as a student and Eagle Scout in his youth. But as a police officer, he had been sued three times for racially motivated misconduct. He was not working alone in these encounters. Each of the times he was accused of acting inappropriately, he was in the presence of other New York Police Department (NYPD) officers.

THE BANNED CHOKE HOLD

Officer Pantaleo used a maneuver known as a choke hold to bring Garner under his control. A choke hold is a physical hold that applies firm and consistent pressure to a person's neck. It often makes breathing difficult.

The NYPD banned the use of choke holds nearly 30 years before Pantaleo used it on Garner. The NYPD knew choke holds were dangerous, but it also knew the choke hold is an effective way to take down a violent suspect. In 1993, the NYPD reminded officers of its ban but also made an exception: a choke hold could be used if an officer believed his or her life was in danger.

The choke hold has not disappeared from practice. The NYPD still frequently uses choke holds. Between 2009 and 2014, New Yorkers made more than 1,100 police choke hold complaints.[5] These were incidents in which civilians claimed the NYPD officers had used the banned maneuver.

THE CELL PHONE VIDEO

Ramsey Orta was a friend of Garner's. When he saw Pantaleo and Damico begin arguing with Garner, Orta took out his smartphone and filmed the encounter. He then sold his video to a newspaper, which quickly made the footage public. Doctors working on Garner's case watched it. Supervisors in charge of Pantaleo and Damico watched it. The American public watched it. Suddenly, Garner's death became the center of a nationwide discussion on police, force, and race.

People reacted to the video in a variety of ways. Some felt it showed an unarmed man being abused by the police. They argued that the police used excessive force and then ignored a man's pleas as he struggled to breathe. Others saw the video in a different way. They noted Garner's large size and anger. They felt the police were acting to protect themselves and others. They said Garner's cries for help could have been an attempt to escape from the police.

The medical examiner in charge of Garner's case said the choke hold and chest compression shown in the video caused Garner's death. The NYPD pledged to investigate what had happened and whether any officers had acted inappropriately. The video also led to a grand jury investigation into the incident. A grand jury is a group of citizens who examine evidence and advise a prosecutor about whether someone should be charged with a crime.

AN ISSUE OF RACE

Race is typically defined as the color of a person's skin. However, race can also include other criteria, such as country of origin and religion. Racism is the belief that certain races are inherently better or worse than others.

Orta's video raised the question of whether Pantaleo and Damico were racist. The officers were white, and Garner was black. Some critics suggested Pantaleo and Damico had treated Garner differently than they would have treated a suspect of another race. Conversely, some people believed the accusations of racism in this case were misguided. They thought the

ARRESTS FOR SMALL CRIMES

Broken windows policing is an approach to reducing crime. It directs police to focus on small but visible crimes and activities. Police are encouraged to arrest or fine people committing crimes such as graffiti and vandalism. The idea is that the public will see these arrests and be reminded of police presence. Then, people will be less likely to commit larger and more serious crimes.

Garner's arrest has been attributed to broken windows policing. His crime of selling loose cigarettes was minor. However, his interaction with the police on the street was public; many people could see him being arrested.

Following Garner's death, neighborhood residents made a memorial at the site of his arrest.

police officers acted appropriately and that Garner's race was not a factor in their behavior. Further, they accused critics of weakening the strength and integrity of law enforcement communities by labeling them as racist.

THE AFTERMATH

Ultimately, the grand jury investigation into the incident found that Pantaleo did not commit a crime when he used a choke hold on Garner. When the verdict was released, protests erupted in several cities across the United States. Protesters shouted their anger that a white police officer had killed an unarmed black man. They cried for justice. They wanted Pantaleo to be punished.

After the incident, both officers were taken off the streets and assigned desk duty. Pantaleo was further punished: the NYPD stripped him of his badge and his gun during the investigation. Soon after the video went public, Pantaleo started receiving death threats. He began living under 24-hour police protection.

The NYPD retrained its police officers. It implemented a three-day course focusing on cultural sensitivity and safe methods to restrain suspects. The course encouraged police officers to think more about how they treated suspects and interacted with their community.

Public opinions remain mixed on what happened, why it happened, and how the NYPD handled Garner's death. The question of whether racism was involved in his death still lingers. In the years following Garner's death, many more incidents of white police officers killing unarmed people of color followed. These deaths have brought the issue of police racism into the public discourse.

| DISCUSSION STARTERS |

- Do you think Garner's race affected his treatment by the police? Why or why not?

- Do you think police officers appreciate being filmed by civilians? Why or why not?

- How do you think the public would have reacted if Pantaleo and Damico had been black?

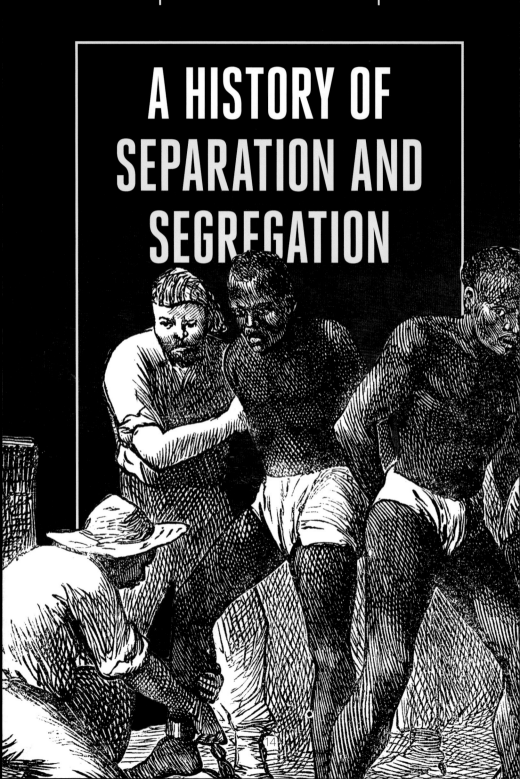

A HISTORY OF SEPARATION AND SEGREGATION

The earliest European settlers who ventured to North America did not arrive to an empty continent. American Indians had long since established thriving civilizations across the land. As Europeans worked to create new settlements on North American soil, they also began a campaign of violence against the Native peoples in the form of wars, slavery, and abuse.

BLACK SLAVERY

Despite harsh winters, disease, and fierce resistance from American Indians, European settlers were able to carve out a home for themselves in North America. In the 1600s, colonists started enslaving and importing people from Africa. They forced these slaves to work the land and perform other manual tasks without pay. Over time, this evolved into a booming slave trade. Between six and seven million enslaved Africans were brought to the United States during the 1700s alone.[1] Slave labor allowed colonists to create a thriving economy based on crops such as cotton and tobacco.

By the 1700s, Great Britain's American colonies were firmly entrenched in racist ideas. When the colonists defeated the British in the Revolutionary War (1775–1783), they won freedom and independence.

But this concept applied only to the white people living in the new country. Black people and American Indians were not considered citizens of the budding nation. The idea that white people were superior to other races was prevalent. Thomas Jefferson, one of the country's Founding Fathers, wrote, "blacks, whether originally a distinct race, or made distinct by time and circumstances, are inferior to the whites."[2]

Slavery was abolished in the northern states by 1804. Those who supported abolition believed slavery was a cruel and unfair practice. However, the leaders of

KU KLUX KLAN

The Ku Klux Klan (KKK) was founded in 1866 in response to the outcome of the Civil War and in reaction to the abolition of slavery. The KKK engaged in acts of violence and intimidation against both black people and their white allies. Its members also targeted Jews, Catholics, and other minority groups. The KKK's primary goal was to establish the supremacy of the white race. Klansmen performed acts of terrorism, often at night and costumed in white robes.

Klan members could be found in nearly every Southern state by 1870. But in 1871, President Ulysses S. Grant signed the Ku Klux Klan Act. This made many of the KKK's acts illegal. However, in some areas, law enforcement officers were actually active members of the KKK.

The KKK still exists today, with active groups in 41 states.[3] In 2014, two Florida police officers were linked with the KKK in their area. The police department immediately fired one of the officers. The other resigned.

Southern states continued to embrace slavery. Slavery became the central issue people fought over in the American Civil War (1861–1865).

In 1863, President Abraham Lincoln issued the Emancipation Proclamation. This wartime announcement stated, "Slaves within any State, or designated part of a state . . . in rebellion . . . shall be then, thenceforward, and forever free."[4] Slavery was officially abolished throughout the country in 1865 with the Thirteenth Amendment to the US Constitution.

THE JIM CROW YEARS

Freedom from slavery did not end racism in the United States. Black Americans, along with other people of color, faced harsh racial discrimination at the hands of white people. In the years following the Civil War, states in the South passed laws known as Black Codes. These laws restricted the activity of black people and often forced them into harsh, yearlong labor contracts with white employers. Black Codes restricted the freedom of formerly enslaved people and kept their status within society below that of white people.

The 1875 Civil Rights Act briefly promised freedom and safety for Americans of all races. It protected all Americans in restaurants, theaters, public transportation, and other public places. However, this law did not have major support, and it was not strongly enforced. In 1883, the Supreme Court found it unconstitutional.

The 1896 Supreme Court case *Plessy v. Ferguson* ruled trains could have separate cars for people of color and white people as long as the cars were equal. This policy came to be known as "separate but equal."[5] The law meant people of color were legally required to use different facilities from whites when such facilities were available. Though these facilities—including restrooms, water fountains, bus seats, and restaurant tables—were supposed to be of equal quality, this was rarely the case.

Prior to the 1950s, laws required people of color to use separate drinking fountains.

"Colored" facilities were often of poor quality compared with white facilities.

Following *Plessy v. Ferguson*, many new laws emerged to enforce the separate but equal ruling. Laws requiring racial segregation came to be known as Jim Crow laws. These state and local laws, which were common throughout the South, were based on the notion that black people and white people should not share the same spaces. Jim Crow laws reinforced the message that black people were inferior.

RACISM AGAINST AMERICAN INDIANS AND ASIANS

American Indians, who had been forced to leave their land and move onto reservations throughout the 1800s, continued to face racism. Some people in the US government referred to the independent cultures of the various tribes as the "Indian Problem." In an attempt to solve this perceived problem, the government set up boarding schools for American Indian children with the goal of eliminating Native cultures. These schools forced children to embrace American customs and forget their heritage. Adult American Indians faced racism as well. They were not allowed in some towns after nightfall. Known as sundown towns, these towns warned American Indians and other minorities that they would face harsh punishment if they did not leave city limits before the sun went down.

Asian Americans have also faced a history of racial discrimination. The Chinese immigrants who helped build railroads in the 1800s were unpopular among many white laborers. Fear of losing work to the immigrant population led to the Chinese Exclusion Act of 1882, which forbade any Chinese immigrants from entering the United States. This act encouraged restrictions against other immigrants, including people from India and Japan.

When the Japanese attacked Pearl Harbor in 1941, the US government responded by forcing all Japanese Americans living on the West Coast into war relocation camps. These prisonlike camps were surrounded by barbed wire. Residents were forced to live in army-style barracks. Guards in high watchtowers held guns and ensured that no one tried

NEW YORK CITY'S FIRST BLACK COP

Samuel Battle was 28 years old when he made history in 1911 by becoming the first black police officer in New York City. He was assigned first to patrol the black San Juan Hill neighborhood. Then, when Harlem's black population grew, he was transferred there. Battle went on to pave the way for other black cops. He became the first black sergeant in 1926, the first black lieutenant in 1935, and finally, the first black parole commissioner in 1941. Despite harassment and mistreatment from white civilians and police, Battle stayed on the force until 1951.

to escape. More than 100,000 Japanese Americans were forced to live inside these camps for the duration of World War II (1939–1945).[6]

LAW ENFORCEMENT'S ROLE

American law enforcement operates to maintain law and order and protect the people. State, federal, and local police are required to uphold all laws. They work to prevent theft, violence, and other types of illegal behavior. However, because of the evolving nature of American race relations, many of the laws police have upheld were racist.

The early roots of modern American policing lie in two sources. In the North, community protection was modeled after the idea of a night watch, in which a group of volunteers enforced the law. The night watch typically did not patrol the streets. Instead, the volunteers waited in a set location for citizens to come to them asking for help. In the South, policing evolved from slave patrols. These were organized groups of white men who patrolled the streets. Their primary focus was to control, discipline, and catch enslaved people who were breaking rules.

Modern policing takes elements from both the night watch and slave patrols in its practice and structure. But today's police do not simply look to the past for lessons on how to function. Modern policing is also constantly evolving to best serve and protect the people.

The first American police department formed in Boston, Massachusetts, in 1838. Other major cities soon followed with departments of their own. Early American police departments worked to maintain order among all citizens. They fought crime, protected the citizens, and maintained order. In the South, they also enforced Jim Crow laws, Black Codes, and segregation.

ATLANTA'S SOUL PATROL

In 1948, the city of Atlanta, Georgia, employed the country's first all-black police squad, nicknamed the Soul Patrol. Though their presence signaled an improvement in race relations in the city, they were not treated equally to their white peers. The Soul Patrol was stationed in a makeshift headquarters located in the basement of the local YMCA. The black officers were not allowed to drive squad cars and were only permitted to patrol black neighborhoods.

LAW ENFORCEMENT AND INTEGRATION

The 1954 Supreme Court case *Brown v. Board of Education* ruled separate but equal was unconstitutional. This ruling meant previously segregated schools had to be integrated. The public reaction to this decision was heated and mixed. In the North, many celebrated the news as an achievement for the civil rights movement. In the South, many white people protested, furious that white schools would be integrated.

For African Americans, the decision was monumental. Black schools had fallen below the standards set for whites; as a result, the education that black children received was inferior, and it often failed to prepare them for gainful employment.

The role law enforcement played in school integration reveals just how complicated race relations were in the 1950s. The first school to integrate was Central High School in Little Rock, Arkansas. On September 4, 1957, nine African Americans tried to enter Central High for their first day of school. National Guard troopers, sent by Arkansas governor Orval Faubus, blocked the students at the door. The governor claimed the troopers were needed to protect the black students. The nine students were forced to return home.

On September 23, the black students tried again. This time, local police officers escorted the students. However, before long, the police deemed the situation too dangerous for the students. White people were rioting outside the school in protest. The police then escorted the students safely away from the school.

On September 25, the Little Rock Nine, as they had become known by the press, were finally able to attend school. This time, President Dwight D. Eisenhower sent in the US Army to protect them.

AN EVOLVING RELATIONSHIP

During the history of the United States, people of color have experienced a variety of behaviors from law enforcement. In the early days of the country, law enforcement officers often contributed to the marginalization of people of color. Police officers enforced laws that required people of color to live in slavery, follow racist curfews, and attend inferior schools. But law enforcement was also instrumental in dismantling some of the country's racist laws and policies. The police protected people of color as laws evolved to recognize the civil rights of all Americans, regardless of their race.

| DISCUSSION STARTERS |

- Do you think stories of police interacting with the Ku Klux Klan have hurt the credibility of law enforcement? Why or why not?

- Why do you think it took until 1954 for the Supreme Court to rule separate but equal was unconstitutional?

- Do you think the historic treatment of black Americans has affected the way they are treated today? Why or why not?

CHAPTER THREE

POLICE AND THE FIGHT FOR EQUAL RIGHTS

In the 1950s and 1960s, activists in the civil rights movement worked to raise awareness of the unequal treatment people of color endured across the United States. These activists peacefully protested the marginalization of minority populations, pointing out how racial and ethnic minorities often faced challenges when voting, seeking a better education, attaining gainful employment, and finding safe housing.

The Civil Rights Act of 1964 ended segregation in public places and made it illegal for employers to discriminate based on a person's race, gender, or religion. The Voting Rights Act of 1965 made it easier for black people to vote, which gave them more political power than ever before. The Civil Rights Act of 1968 made it illegal for people who were selling or renting property to discriminate based on race, sex, or religion.

The laws passed in the 1960s promised a brighter future for people of color. However, the civil rights movement faced heavy resistance from many Americans who did not want to see the end of segregation. Whereas the civil rights movement was characterized by nonviolence, the resistance against it—enforced by both civilians and the police—was at times extremely violent.

The role law enforcement played in the civil rights movement was complex and varied. In some areas, police officers were instrumental in the success of protests, marches, and ultimately the passage of new laws. In other areas, law enforcement officers contributed to violence against people of color and supported the resistance against the civil rights movement.

BLOODY SUNDAY

Selma, Alabama, was the scene of one of the most violent clashes between law enforcement and civil rights activists. On March 7, 1965, hundreds of protesters marched to raise awareness of the resistance black voters faced. Their march was interrupted by Alabama state troopers and local police, who ordered the marchers to

RESEARCHING RACIAL VIOLENCE

In 1967, President Lyndon B. Johnson asked Illinois governor Otto Kerner to lead an investigation into the spike in racially motivated violent unrest sweeping the nation. Kerner's 426-page report, issued the following year, warned, "Our nation is moving toward two societies, one black, one white—separate and unequal." The report blamed "white racism" for the racial violence that was occurring in urban centers with alarming frequency.[1]

The Kerner Report offered solutions to solve the racial divide. It urged the government to launch programs to help black Americans achieve success. These included creating new jobs, constructing new housing, and dissolving the urban ghettos.

turn around. When the marchers refused, the troopers and police violently attacked them. Film footage of the day, which became known as Bloody Sunday, was televised around the world.

Much of the American public was outraged at the images of police brutality. Civil rights leader Martin Luther King Jr. encouraged his supporters to go to Selma for another march. President Lyndon B. Johnson knew the importance of the march. He also knew he could not count on local police to protect the marchers. On March 21, thousands of marchers repeated the trek across

Civil rights protesters gather outside a church in Selma, Alabama, to begin their march.

Selma. This time, they were under the protection of the US Army and Alabama National Guard officers, sent by President Johnson himself.

FROM CIVIL RIGHTS TO BLACK POWER

In the years following the civil rights movement, some black activists grew frustrated with the nonviolent tactics used by King and his followers. Stokely Carmichael was an African American who believed activists needed to try something new to achieve their goals. He founded his own political party, called the Lowndes County Freedom Party. Carmichael's party didn't last long, but the logo he chose did: it was a snarling black panther. The party's slogan was Black Power. The logo and slogan captured the strength and resilience of black resistance.

In 1966, Huey Newton and Bobby Seale started the Black Panther Party for Self-Defense in Oakland, California. At first, the Black Panthers existed as a street patrol organization. At the time, police brutality against black people was common. Groups of Black Panthers walked black neighborhoods and looked for the police. If they observed an African American being arrested, the Panthers stood by to make sure the police did not commit any abuses. Members of the Black Panther Party exercised their constitutional right to bear arms.

The Black Panthers' public display of their guns had a major impact on both law enforcement and the black community. For law enforcement, it was often seen as a threat of violence, as police worried that they could be shot if their actions were misinterpreted. For many in the black community, the guns represented empowerment.

Over time, the Black Panther Party evolved to become more than a neighborhood patrol. It became a revolutionary social group that encouraged African Americans to fight economic oppression, arm themselves, and help their communities.

Black Panthers made no secret about the fact that they carried guns.

WHITE FLIGHT AND URBAN GHETTOS

The 1960s and 1970s saw a wave of white flight, a phenomenon in which millions of white Americans left urban centers and moved to homes in the suburbs. Banks and lawmakers aided white flight by creating policies that segregated suburban communities. Banks, for example, made it extremely difficult for black people to obtain loans for houses in certain neighborhoods. Some housing developers even said only "members of the Caucasian race" could live in their properties.[2] Though the Civil Rights Act of 1968 made this illegal, housing discrimination continued to occur.

Along with white flight came urban decay, which was characterized by the weakening of urban infrastructures. As wealthy white people left,

THE PROJECTS

Public housing projects are rental apartments the government makes available to people with low incomes, people with disabilities, and the elderly. Many early housing projects, established in the 1930s, were racially segregated. African Americans often faced discrimination when trying to rent or buy homes in white neighborhoods, leaving many with no choice but to stay in the projects.

In some cities, nearly all of the public housing residents are black. In Detroit, Michigan, for instance, 99 percent of the people living in public housing were black as of 2013. In New Orleans, Louisiana, and Washington, DC, the number was 98 percent.[3]

cities lost the income tax these residents had paid. This tax money went to the suburbs instead. Losing tax money often meant city schools, hospitals, and other public places suffered. City centers tended to have higher rates of poverty, mental illness, and crime than the suburbs did. As a result, the police typically had a large and visible presence in urban areas. Police forces were often predominantly white, and urban areas usually had high numbers of people of color, creating the perception of a racial divide.

THE DRUG EPIDEMIC

In the 1980s and 1990s, relationships between law enforcement and people of color continued to evolve. These years saw drug epidemics sweep through cities across the United States. Street drugs such as heroin and crack cocaine were cheap, highly addictive, and dangerous. This drug abuse crisis affected people of all races, but it was predominantly seen among communities of color.

Neighborhoods where drug abuse is common typically have higher crime rates than areas where drug abuse is rare. People who are using drugs often act recklessly, irresponsibly, or violently, and they may commit crimes. To maintain order, police departments started to closely

Suspected drug dealers were held at gunpoint while officers raided a house in Washington, DC, in 1989.

monitor areas with high levels of drug abuse. This often meant officers were patrolling minority neighborhoods.

Many Americans were worried about the drug crisis, which led President Ronald Reagan and his wife, Nancy, to make the fight against drugs a top priority. One of their methods involved shifting the way drug abuse was discussed. Rather than thinking of it as a health crisis, the

Reagans encouraged people to think of it as an issue for the judicial system.

In 1986, the Anti-Drug Abuse Act became law, requiring longer prison sentences for offenses involving street drugs such as crack cocaine. African Americans were especially affected by the criminalization of drug abuse. By the early 1990s, black people accounted for 12 percent of the US population but made up 40 percent of all drug-related arrests.[4] Black people were approximately five times as likely to be arrested for a drug offense as were white people who had committed the same crime.

CRIME IN COMMUNITIES OF COLOR

All across the United States, in cities and rural areas alike, minority communities experienced higher rates of crime than white communities. The causes for the racial disparity in crime rates are hard to identify. Some experts believe high rates of poverty in black communities have led to high rates of crime; they believe the crime is a result of poverty, not race. Others say the way black and white people are treated by law enforcement might make these crime rates an inaccurate reflection of the actual situation. For example, black communities tend to be policed more rigorously than white communities—so if a black person and white person each commit a crime, the black person is more likely to be arrested. In addition, black people are more likely to be convicted than white people accused of the same crime.

The separation and marginalization of people of color had many outcomes. One effect of this racial division was that people of color and white police often saw each other as adversaries. This tension, often described as an us-versus-them mentality, created an atmosphere of mutual distrust. As a result, police officers faced major challenges when doing their job.

DISTRUST AND ANGER

At the end of the 1900s, the relationship between law enforcement and many people of color remained strained. Racial and ethnic minorities, especially African Americans, were more likely to be approached, questioned, and arrested by police than white people were. This created a social tension in many communities, with African Americans and the police feeling hostile toward one another.

One issue that contributed to the poor relationships between civilians and law enforcement was the fact that police forces were often predominantly white. This lack of diversity in law enforcement led many civilians, particularly minorities, to have a poor perception of the police.

Distrust of the police greatly weakens the ability of law enforcement officials to do their jobs effectively. When the public loses trust in the police, they may stop thinking of the police as authority figures. This mentality makes it less likely

RAPPERS MAKE THEIR VOICES HEARD

In 1988, hip-hop group N.W.A released its album *Straight Outta Compton*. The album, which went on to sell more than three million copies, centers on the theme of gang violence in Los Angeles, California. The second track on the album, entitled "F*** tha Police," was written after N.W.A members were harassed by Los Angeles police officers. The song's provocative lyrics created a major controversy and prompted an FBI investigation into the group. However, the song also brought the issue of police brutality into the national spotlight.

that people will follow police orders. It also creates an environment in which civilians may become fearful of law enforcement personnel.

Responding to critiques that police departments should look more like the people they protect, law enforcement departments across the nation began to diversify in the late 1980s and early 1990s. More women and people of color became law enforcement officers. Many observers hoped these developments would help heal the rift between minority communities and the police. However, others were skeptical that these changes would help.

| DISCUSSION STARTERS |

- How do you think the civil rights movement and Black Power movement affected the relationship between African Americans and law enforcement?

- What effect do you think the Black Panther Party's use of guns had on the way black people were perceived by both civilians and law enforcement?

- How did housing segregation contribute to crime and safety?

- Do you think city police work changed after white flight? If so, how do you think it changed?

CHAPTER FOUR

TO SERVE AND PROTECT

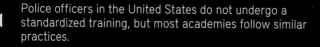

In many countries, police operate under a single, national umbrella. However, police forces in the United States are organized differently. They fall under federal, local, and state controls. This fragmentation is purposeful. Founders of American law enforcement did not want an all-powerful federal police force. Another reason for the division is that Americans generally believe local police are best at handling local problems.

Police departments in the United States are structured to ensure that supervisors monitor and oversee junior officers. Though structures vary across state, local, and federal departments, most follow a similar pattern. A police chief, director, or superintendent runs the force. Under that person are senior officers. At the bottom of the structure are troopers, deputies, cadets, and junior officers.

Training to become a police officer typically involves classroom lessons on basic law enforcement principles, along with hands-on practice and simulations. Because each state and jurisdiction has different training standards for police officers, there is no set requirement all American police officers must achieve. However, many common requirements exist in training academies across the nation. Ninety-nine percent of police academy trainees are taught to use a firearm. On average, they spend 60 hours on this skill.[1]

Other topics frequently taught in police academies include criminal law, self-defense, and basic first aid. Ninety-eight percent of academies teach trainees about ethics and integrity. Trainees spend an average of eight hours on this topic. Ninety-five percent of academies focus on cultural diversity. Police trainees typically receive eight hours of diversity education.[2]

Today, some police departments are spending extra time retraining their officers on matters of racial and cultural sensitivity. Programs such as Blue Courage offer a three-day intensive training program for active police officers to learn how to better serve their

WHEN A SUSPECT POSES A SIGNIFICANT THREAT

In 1974, white police officer Elton Hymon shot and killed Edward Garner, a black teen fleeing the scene of a robbery. Hymon admitted he was "reasonably sure" Garner was unarmed.[3] However, the officer still used deadly force to prevent the suspect's escape. The slain teen's father brought the issue to federal court, claiming his son's civil rights had been violated.

In 1985, the US Supreme Court ruled on the case. The court decided police must not use deadly force unless they have "probable cause to believe that the suspect poses a significant threat of death or serious physical injury to the officer or others."[4] The court's ruling appeared to restrict police use of deadly force. However, Hymon was never charged in Edward Garner's death.

communities and become aware of their own feelings about different groups of people.

POLICING THE POLICE

When police officers are accused of acting inappropriately or committing a crime, they are subject to an internal review in which their police force will determine whether they have violated police regulations. Accused officers may also be charged in criminal court for their actions. In addition, victims may sue officers in civil court.

American police departments strive to ensure that their officers act appropriately and treat citizens fairly. This is especially true with regard to incidents involving

Despite officers' training, routine events such as traffic stops sometimes escalate into more serious incidents.

accusations of racism. Offending officers may be fined, disciplined, or even fired. In 2015, a white police officer in Georgia was accused of making racial remarks to a black driver during a traffic stop. The officer was punished and reassigned to a different area, and the officer's supervisor wrote the driver a letter of apology. Occasionally, police officers are also subject to the criminal justice system. When a Hispanic police officer beat a black man during a Michigan traffic stop, the officer received a sentence of 13 months to 10 years in prison for his crime.[5]

Not all police are punished for racially motivated actions. In 2011 and 2012, several police officers in San Francisco, California, sent each other racist text messages that included racial slurs and calls to violence against minorities. One message referred to an African American, writing, "Get ur pocket gun. Keep it available in case the monkey returns to his roots. Its not against the law to put an animal down."[6] Another message referred to people of mixed race as "half-breeds" and called them an "abomination of nature."[7] The officers' police chief said, "It makes me sick to my stomach to even have these guys around."[8] However, the officers ultimately went unpunished; the statute of limitations required any investigation into an officer's behavior to take place within

RACE DISPARITY

Diversity in a police force has been shown to improve police-community relationships. A 2015 report from the Department of Justice and US Equal Employment Opportunity Commission found that diversity in a police force increases the level of trust between law enforcement and the public. The report notes this "basic trust" can help in "defusing tension, investigating and solving crimes, and creating a system where citizens believe that they can rely on their police departments and receive fair treatment."[10]

However, in many areas, the number of white officers is more than 30 percent higher than the number of white residents in the community. This disparity can negatively affect the ability of police to do their jobs. It can also contribute to civilians' poor perception of police.

**North Charleston,
South Carolina:**
White residents: 38%
White officers: 80%

Dellwood, Missouri:
White residents: 18%
White officers: 94%

Stone Park, Illinois:
White residents: 8%
White officers: 83%[11]

a year, and the police department took too long to address the misconduct. Some of the officers quit the force, but others remained on duty.

Police officers are sometimes called on to use lethal force. In 2013, law enforcement officers were involved in more than 450 "justifiable homicides."[9] Law enforcement homicides are considered justified if they are necessary for the survival of the officer, the prevention of the suspect's escape, or the safety of the public. If lethal force is used in a questionable situation, an officer might be indicted on murder charges. However, police officers are rarely indicted for shooting deaths. In a typical year, only four or five police are indicted for on-duty shootings.[12] Many laws protect police officers and support their ability to make snap decisions in difficult and dangerous circumstances. In the rare instances in which they are accused, police officers are almost never found guilty of murder. Between 2005 and 2016, only 13 officers were convicted of murder or manslaughter for on-duty shootings.[13]

EXTREME LETHAL FORCE

Police are sometimes called on to disrupt protests or other gatherings. Usually, they rely on nonlethal tactics. Verbal commands are a simple tool for law enforcement. Officers can simply use a bullhorn or shout to the crowds to disperse. When this does not work, police can escalate their tactics. In extreme cases, they may turn to more forceful means, such as water cannons, rubber bullets, tear gas, or concussion grenades. These tools are not meant to be lethal. Police use them to subdue or disperse people.

In 1985, the police force in Philadelphia, Pennsylvania, used excessive lethal force. That year, a radical black liberation group called MOVE occupied a house in a busy Philadelphia neighborhood. The name *MOVE* was not an acronym; rather, it signified the group's activism. MOVE

WHEN TROUBLED COPS KILL

Some police officers show signs of trouble before they act out violently on the job. For instance, Officer Pantaleo had been sued three times for misconduct before using a choke hold on Eric Garner. Police departments across the United States are working to better identify warning signs of officers who may act out violently in the future. Some departments have begun sharing data on police behavior. They hope experts will be able to analyze this data to determine what types of actions or attitudes predict violent behaviors.

members worked out of the house to encourage people to fight racism, protest police brutality, and advocate for animal rights, among other causes. MOVE and the Philadelphia police had a violent history. In 1978, MOVE members had killed a police officer in a shootout. Nine MOVE members had each received long prison sentences for the officer's death.

In May 1985, Philadelphia police responded to neighborhood complaints about MOVE's residential headquarters. The activists had been broadcasting loud lectures at all hours of the day and night from their rooftop. Police arrived on the scene with warrants, but MOVE members did not allow them inside. Soon, gunfire erupted from inside the MOVE house. Approximately 500 police officers responded with 10,000 bullets in the

A member of MOVE stands guard in front of the group's headquarters in 1977.

course of 90 minutes.[14] The police also used fire hoses and tear gas. Still, the MOVE members did not surrender.

The police commissioner ordered his forces to bomb the MOVE house from a helicopter. The bomb destroyed the house and started a huge blaze. In all, the bomb and fire destroyed 61 homes and killed 11 people, including five children. A review commission later investigated the incident and found the police actions "grossly negligent" and "unconscionable."[15] Even so, none of the people responsible for the bombing or fire were ever prosecuted.

UNARMED POLICE

In some countries, most police officers do not carry firearms. The United Kingdom, Norway, Ireland, New Zealand, and Iceland permit officers to carry guns only on special assignments. These police forces are still able to maintain peace, even in heavily armed societies. In Iceland, for example, approximately one-third of the population owns guns for hunting.

British police are happy without guns; 82 percent of officers report they do not want to carry firearms. Greater Manchester Chief Constable Sir Peter Fahy said in 2012, "Sadly we know from the experience in America and other countries that having armed officers certainly does not mean . . . police officers do not end up getting shot."[16]

POLICE PERSPECTIVE

Police officers serve their communities and strive to uphold the law. But they are also human. Police officers experience fear, anger, and compassion, just as civilians do. Their training prepares them to handle stressful situations safely and calmly, but sometimes police officers make mistakes. These mistakes can become extremely complicated and weighty when they occur between a white officer and a civilian of color.

Former US attorney general Eric Holder, who is black, touched on the complex nature of police and race. "Communities of color don't understand what it means to be a police officer, the fear that police officers have in just being on the streets," he said.[17] Holder and other legal experts have emphasized that a better understanding of the police perspective can help communities bridge the gap between civilians and law enforcement.

| DISCUSSION STARTERS |

- Why do you think American police departments do not all use the same training methods?

- How do you think the MOVE bombing affected the way people in Philadelphia thought about the police?

- Do you think police officers should carry guns? Why or why not?

CHAPTER FIVE

WALKING WHILE BLACK

Modern police departments use various protocols and best practices to do their jobs as effectively as possible. Officers are trained to identify risk, remain vigilant, and act quickly. Their training is designed to de-escalate violent situations, protecting both themselves and the citizens. For example, many law enforcement officers have learned protocol for how best to approach a person standing on the edge of a bridge. To prevent that person's suicide, the officers are taught to engage calmly in conversation. Years of experience have taught them that tackling a would-be bridge jumper is ineffective and ruins trust between the officer and the civilian. This protocol exists to protect the officer, prevent the suicide, and ultimately change the jumper's behavior.

STOP AND FRISK

Occasionally, some police protocols evolve into behaviors that, according to critics, target people of color. In 1990, for example, police in New York City adopted a program called Stop and Frisk. Stop and Frisk allowed officers to interview and frisk people on the street to determine if they were carrying weapons or other illegal items, such as drugs. The officers had to have reasonable suspicion that the person had been engaged in criminal activity.

They also had to have reasonable suspicion that the person was armed and dangerous. Each time officers conducted a Stop and Frisk, they were supposed to record details of the interaction. While Stop and Frisk was intended to apply to all people, police records show it disproportionately targeted black and Hispanic men.

In the years after Stop and Frisk was implemented, serious and violent crimes in New York City dropped to historic lows. Some people believed Stop and Frisk was responsible for this drastic decrease. Supporters of Stop and Frisk applauded the

FREDDIE GRAY AND THE BALTIMORE POLICE

In 2015, police in Baltimore, Maryland, arrested 25-year-old Freddie Gray for running from them. They later learned Gray, an African American, had a knife. Officers loaded Gray into the back of a police van and drove him to the police station. During the ride, Gray sustained serious spinal injuries. After arriving at the police station, Gray was immediately transported to a hospital. He fell into a coma and later died.

Shortly after news of Gray's death reached the public, activists in Baltimore began protesting what they suspected was an incident of police brutality. They demanded information about what had happened to Gray. As details began to emerge, these protests grew violent. After Gray's funeral, Baltimore erupted in riots.

An investigation into Gray's death failed to prove exactly what happened. The arresting officers admitted they violated protocol by not buckling Gray into the van. Many media outlets suggested the driver of the van intentionally drove erratically to injure Gray. None of the officers involved in Gray's death were found guilty of crimes.

Activists, including civil rights leader Reverend Al Sharpton, *center right*, march against Stop and Frisk during a 2012 protest in New York City.

program's ability to stop crime before it occurred. Critics of Stop and Frisk argue that this was coincidental. They point to the fact that the entire nation, including cities that did not promote Stop and Frisk, saw drops in violent crime around this time. They also note that New York's drop in crime began before the spike of Stop and Frisks.

In 2013, a New York judge ruled the Stop and Frisk program was carried out in a way that violated the Constitution. The judge pointed out how police were

targeting people of color. She said Stop and Frisk had become "a policy of indirect racial profiling."[1] The judge did not order police to stop using Stop and Frisk. Rather, she directed police to change the way they utilized the practice to ensure they were not discriminating against any civilians. However, the US Court of Appeals for the Second Circuit overruled her decision. The NYPD later settled the case by paying money to some of the people who felt they had been mistreated.

RACIAL PROFILING

Racial profiling is a type of racial discrimination. It occurs when law enforcement targets a person based on race, rather than other factors, for suspicion of crime.

Racial profiling is unconstitutional. The Fourteenth Amendment to the US Constitution promises equal protection to all Americans, regardless of race. Racial profiling is also ineffective. Police who engage in racial profiling alienate themselves from the community and create an atmosphere of distrust. A study of the Los Angeles Police Department found that minority groups who felt they had been racially profiled by the police in the past continued to fear and mistrust them in the present. This fear and mistrust undermines police authority. When people are afraid of the police, they are less likely to turn to them for protection.

Today, the phrase *walking while black* refers to police racial profiling. It is a word play on the illegal activity *driving while intoxicated*, and it refers to the notion that some black people are treated as though they are breaking the law simply by walking outside.

Many political leaders are urging American police to eliminate racial profiling. In 2016, President Barack Obama said, "We can and must do better to institute the best practices that reduce the appearance or reality of racial bias in law enforcement."[2] Obama's comment pointed to the importance of both the actions of the police and the way those actions are interpreted by the public. Both of these affect the relationship between the public and the police.

Identifying instances of police racial profiling can be extremely difficult. It can be hard to determine which stops are legitimate and without prejudice and which are the result of an officer's racial bias.

DOWN TO THE DATA

Harvard professor Roland G. Fryer Jr. wanted to do something about the deaths of unarmed black men at the hands of police. "Protesting is not my thing," said Fryer, who is black. "But data is my thing."[3] He and his team of researchers spent 3,000 hours poring over police report data to learn just how race affects police interactions.

Fryer was surprised by his findings. He learned that black people are more likely to be physically touched, handcuffed, brought to the ground, or pepper sprayed than are white people. However, he also learned that police shootings are not influenced by racial bias. Black people, according to Fryer's findings, were no more likely to be shot by police than white people were.

BLACK-ON-BLACK CRIME

Some observers claim racial profiling is not behind the high numbers of black and Hispanic arrests. Rather, they say, these populations commit crimes that make them susceptible to arrest. Political commentator Bill O'Reilly argues that minority communities, especially black

#DWB

In many cities across the United States, black people are pulled over for traffic violations far more often than white people are. This disparity has led to the hashtag #DWB or #DrivingWhileBlack. In Greensboro, North Carolina, black people are twice as likely to have their cars searched by police, compared with white people.[6] However, statistics show that police find drugs or weapons more often when a driver is white. Greensboro police note most black people in Greensboro live in high-crime areas. And because police patrol high-crime areas more than low-crime neighborhoods, black people are stopped more often.

communities, are not being unfairly targeted. He has likened racial profiling to criminal profiling, noting that the police patrol high-crime communities, regardless of their racial makeup. In a 2015 show, O'Reilly stated, "it's not white on black crime that's the problem. It's black on black crime that is causing social chaos."[4]

The topic of black-on-black crime often comes up in discussions of racial profiling. Former New York mayor Rudy Giuliani weighed in on the issue in a controversial 2014 interview. "Ninety-three percent of blacks are killed by other blacks," he said. Giuliani went on to defend the police, saying, "White police officers wouldn't be there if you weren't killing each other."[5]

Giuliani's critics said his comments contributed to the perception that black people are dangerous and that police officers operate without racial bias. His statement did not address the issues of inequality that lead to poor communities, the critics said. They emphasized how living in poor communities can make people feel desperate—and desperate situations can foster desperate behaviors.

NAVIGATING MURKY WATERS

Understanding the role race plays in police interactions can be difficult. The circumstances change from situation to situation. Although discussions about race and police are often heated, many observers agree that citizens and police must work harder to strengthen their bond. In 2016, President Obama said the country is "not even close" to resolving its issues with race, the police, and force.[7]

2016 VICE-PRESIDENTIAL DEBATE

During a 2016 vice-presidential debate, the candidates talked about many topics, including immigration, taxes, and national security. They also discussed police and race. Future vice-president Mike Pence, Donald Trump's Republican running mate, said he thought Americans should stop responding to police shootings in ways that "accuse law enforcement of implicit bias or institutional racism."[8] Pence did not think it was fair to portray an entire group of people as racially biased. Tim Kaine, Hillary Clinton's Democratic running mate, said he thought discussing racial bias was an important step in improving relationships between police and the communities they serve. "If you're afraid to have the discussion, it will never happen," Kaine said.[9]

This dynamic was further complicated when Donald Trump won the 2016 presidential election. Many people in law enforcement had criticized Obama, saying he was not supportive enough of police; in contrast, President Trump has been a strong supporter of law enforcement. In turn, many police officers have supported Trump as well. Trump has spoken in favor of controversial police policies such as Stop and Frisk, but he is hopeful that the relationship between the police and the public can improve under his presidency. In a 2016 interview, he said, "It's a very, very sad situation and hopefully it can be healed."[10]

| DISCUSSION STARTERS |

- How do you think clearly defined police protocols benefit police officers? How do these protocols benefit civilians?

- How has black-on-black crime affected the way some people think about police violence?

- How do you think police officers can use Stop and Frisk without engaging in racial profiling?

- How does policing affect electoral politics?

A plainclothes white officer frisks a black man in New York City.

CHAPTER SIX

THE ROLE OF FEAR

Law enforcement exists to protect communities.
However, police are less effective when citizens are
fearful, distrustful, or antagonistic. For law enforcement
to function as designed, the police must protect the
people, and the people must respect the police.

American police and the communities they serve have
long struggled to find this balance. Incidents of racial
profiling, misconduct, discrimination, and excessive force
are highly visible reminders that some police officers are
flawed. These incidents make it difficult for many people
to trust the police. On the other hand, many police
officers feel they are being seen unfairly because of the
actions of a few.

A FEW BAD APPLES

Modern police are facing a crisis. In 2015, only 52 percent
of Americans reported feeling confident in the police. The
number had not been so low since 1993.[1] The previous
year, in 1992, Los Angeles had erupted in riots following
the not-guilty verdicts of four white police officers who
beat Rodney King, a black motorist.

One explanation for the sweeping lack of confidence
in the police is known as the bad apple theory. This theory
acknowledges that a few bad apples, or misbehaving

police, exist. These bad apples spoil the reputation of the rest of the force, despite the fact that a vast majority of officers do not engage in criminal behavior.

The bad apple theory, though popular, fails to explain incidents in which police misbehavior is covered up or goes unpunished. In the 1970s and 1980s, for example, a group of white Chicago detectives regularly tortured and abused black suspects to force them to falsely confess to crimes. Jon Burge led the ring of detectives and encouraged their behavior. Burge was responsible for burning, beating, and electrocuting more than 100 black

MUSLIMS AND SIKHS AFTER 9/11

Following the terrorist attacks of September 11, 2001, American Sikhs and Muslims have suffered prejudice, discrimination, and even violence at the hands of both civilians and law enforcement. In July 2015, a Muslim woman raced to catch her train at a busy Chicago station. When police officers asked her to stop, she kept running. The police tackled the woman and charged her with reckless conduct and resisting arrest. She was later found not guilty.

In 2016, a Sikh man in Pennsylvania walked into a mall wearing an ornamental knife called a kirpan. The kirpan is one of the five articles of the Sikh faith, and Sikhs must wear them at all times. The knife frightened onlookers, who called the police and reported a "Muslim man" walking around the mall with a "sword." When police surrounded the man and searched him, they discovered the kirpan. The incident made the Sikh man "embarrassed, humiliated, (and) ashamed." The local police captain insisted that the people who reported the Sikh man acted appropriately. "They did the right thing," he said.[2]

men in custody.[3] Burge was not fired until 1993, long after many in the department knew about his actions. In the years since the public learned about Burge, the Chicago Police Department has struggled to regain community trust.

Sometimes police departments punish misbehaving officers publicly and severely. This sends a message to the public that police misconduct is not tolerated. In 2016, a white Pennsylvania police officer posted a selfie on a social media account along with the caption "I'm the law today nigga." The officer was immediately fired. The local police chief reminded the public, "We have more integrity than that in this department."[4]

COMPLAINTS AGAINST CHICAGO POLICE

The Chicago Police Department receives thousands of complaints each year about police abuse. A study of the complaints received between 2011 and 2015 shows very few of these complaints result in punishments for officers. Only 2.6 percent of the Chicago complaints led to disciplinary action for police. This number is below many other cities, which range between 6 and 20 percent.

Of the 29,000 police complaints that Chicagoans filed in this same period, black people lodged more than 10,000 of them. Even fewer of these complaints led to discipline for the police. Only 1.6 percent of African Americans' complaints resulted in punishment.[5]

EXCESSIVE FORCE

Police are often called on to use physical force to subdue suspects. Officers may have to use reasonable force to hold people's arms behind their backs or push them onto the ground. Reasonable force is legal, but excessive force is not. Excessive force is any use of force that exceeds what is necessary to subdue a suspect.

Excessive force is a difficult concept to teach. Some police jurisdictions have some moves that are prohibited, such as the choke hold used to subdue Eric Garner. But beyond illegal moves, it can be difficult to explain what is and is not an acceptable use of force. For example, a

The majority of excessive force complaints do not end in punishment for the accused officers.

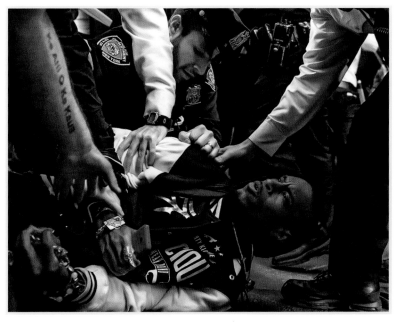

particular maneuver might subdue one suspect but have little effect on another. That is why each police officer must determine how much force to use on each suspect. Other factors complicate the matter further. If a suspect is acting violently toward the officer, bystanders, or himself, an officer may act with as much force as he or she finds necessary.

Many police officers are instructed to use a force continuum to determine the level of force necessary in any given situation. They start with verbal requests and lead up to more aggressive tactics—from demands to chemical sprays to physical force and finally to lethal force.

WHEN THE POLICE ARE SCARED OF THE PEOPLE

Police officers are trained to stay calm and rational during all types of interactions. However, adrenaline and fear can affect their judgment or behavior. Civil rights attorney Constance Rice studied the role fear plays in police violence. "Cops can get into a state of mind where they're scared to death," Rice said.[6]

In August 2014, an incident in Ferguson, Missouri, highlighted the complex role fear plays in policing. Officer Darren Wilson, who is white, shot and killed Michael Brown, an unarmed black man who had robbed a convenience store earlier in the day. Wilson later testified that he thought Brown looked like "a demon." Even after Wilson had drawn his gun, Brown did not seem afraid. This affected Wilson. He remembered thinking, "It looked like [Brown] was almost bulking up to run through the shots, like it was making him mad that I'm shooting at him."[7]

Rice noted that fear can bring out subconscious, buried fears about race. "I have known cops who haven't had a racist bone in their bodies and in fact had adopted black children, they went to black churches on the weekend, and these are the white cops," she said. "But you know what they had in their minds that made them act out and beat a black suspect

FORCE CONTINUUM

Many police departments instruct officers to follow a force continuum when interacting with civilians. This continuum begins with little or no force and escalates to use of physical force. At the end of the continuum is lethal force. Below is an example of a force continuum police may be taught:

- Police presence. This involves no force at all. Mere police presence is often enough to affect the desired behaviors in people.
- Calm verbal requests, such as "Can I see your license?"
- Loud verbal commands, such as "Stop!"
- Soft bodily force, such as grasping a suspect's arm.
- Hard bodily force, such as punches or kicks.
- Nonlethal force, such as pepper spray, baton strikes, or Taser use.
- Lethal force, such as the use of a firearm.

Demonstrators gather in Ferguson, Missouri, following the shooting death of Michael Brown.

unwarrantedly? They had fear. They were afraid of black men."[8]

UNDERSTANDING BOTH SIDES' FEAR

Many activists and political leaders have urged Americans to try to understand both sides of this issue. They emphasize that both the police and their communities struggle to cope with fear after police killings.

Author and former basketball star Kareem Abdul-Jabbar has written at length about the complexities of race and policing. He acknowledges that some people see police officers as "uniformed terrorists."[9] But he also encourages readers to see the police as heroes, especially those who work to enact change in their departments. He asks readers to consider "whether or not the police in America are themselves an endangered minority who are also discriminated against based on their color—blue."[10]

THE BIOLOGY OF FEAR

Fear has a profound effect on the body. When a person becomes afraid, the body releases stress hormones such as adrenaline. These hormones affect the way the brain works, making it difficult for the brain to make rational decisions. Instead, the brain reacts instantly. It triggers a response to either fight or flee. These responses are rarely the result of careful thought. Rather, they are instinctual. Understanding the biomechanics of fear can illuminate some ways that police and civilians behave during confrontations.

| DISCUSSION STARTERS |

- How do you think fear affects an officer's ability to make decisions?

- How do you think fear changes the way people behave around the police?

- How do you think the attacks of September 11, 2001, affected race relations in the United States?

BLACK LIVES MATTER

In February 2012, neighborhood watch volunteer George Zimmerman was driving through his community in Sanford, Florida. He began following a black 17-year-old named Trayvon Martin, who was walking home from a convenience store. Zimmerman, a 28-year-old part-Hispanic man, believed Martin was acting suspiciously, so he chased Martin on foot. The two got into a fight. It ended with Zimmerman shooting and killing Martin, who was unarmed. Zimmerman went to trial, and the jury found him not guilty. A controversial Florida law, known as the Stand Your Ground law, allows citizens to use deadly force to protect themselves.

In response to Zimmerman's acquittal, three black activists founded a social movement called Black Lives Matter. They started out using the hashtag #blacklivesmatter on Facebook. Soon, they set up Black Lives Matter Tumblr and Twitter accounts for people to use and share stories. Before long, the words *Black Lives Matter* began appearing on signs at protests and marches. Black Lives Matter activists began organizing meetings, lectures, parades, and protests to raise awareness of their cause. The guiding principles of the movement encourage peaceful dialogue and loving engagement.

Today, the Black Lives Matter movement campaigns against violence and racism toward black people, and it works to educate the public on the racism and bias that contribute to abuse. Members of the movement have been active in protests against police shootings of unarmed black people such as Tamir Rice. Twelve-year-old Rice was shot and killed by police in Cleveland, Ohio, in 2014 after police mistook his toy gun for a real weapon.

ALL LIVES MATTER

In response to the Black Lives Matter movement, a countermovement called All Lives Matter was formed. All Lives Matter emphasizes that race should not be a factor in mourning the death of an innocent person.

JESSE WILLIAMS'S BET SPEECH

In 2016, actor and producer Jesse Williams received a humanitarian award from Black Entertainment Television (BET). His acceptance speech focused on racial disparities and the police killings of unarmed black people. "Police somehow manage to de-escalate, disarm, and not kill white people every day," he said. "So what's going to happen is we are going to have equal rights and justice in our own country or we will restructure their function and ours."[1]

Williams's speech was met with a variety of responses. The audience at the award show gave him a standing ovation. However, a user on Change.org soon formed a petition to get the actor fired from the show *Grey's Anatomy*. The petition accused Williams of "racist, hate speech against law enforcement and white people."[2] Shonda Rhimes, the show's creator and executive producer, assured the public Williams would not be fired.

Demonstrators make their voices heard during a march held in the aftermath of the fatal police shootings in July 2016.

Critics of All Lives Matter describe the movement as either antiblack or misguided. They believe All Lives Matter ignores the systemic racism that has led to the high number of black deaths at the hands of police. Actor and writer Arthur Chu took to Twitter to explain why he believed All Lives Matter was misguided. He joked, "Do people who change #blacklivesmatter to #alllivesmatter run through a cancer fundraiser yelling 'THERE ARE OTHER DISEASES TOO[?]'"[3]

While campaigning for president, Democratic candidate Hillary Clinton also used the phrase "All Lives Matter" during a speech at a black church in Missouri.[4] She later clarified her meaning and stated, "Black lives matter. . . . Everyone in this country should stand firmly behind that."[5]

DALLAS SHOOTINGS

In July 2016, a peaceful demonstration in Dallas, Texas, turned deadly. Protesters had gathered to raise awareness of two recent police shootings of black men in Minnesota and Louisiana. Dallas police officers surrounded the protest to ensure the demonstration remained safe.

Micah Johnson, a 25-year-old African American, was upset about the recent police shootings. He set out to kill as many white police officers as possible. Shooting from various concealed positions, he killed five white police officers and injured seven more. The next day, police cornered Johnson and killed him using a robotic explosive device.

BLACK LIVES MATTER AND CRIME

In 2015, murder rates in the nation's 50 largest cities jumped by 17 percent.[6] Critics said this crime surge was the result of the Black Lives Matter movement. They claimed Black Lives Matter had created an atmosphere in which police were reluctant to stop individuals for fear of being accused of racism. Bill O'Reilly explained this phenomenon simply, saying, "When you fail to police proactively, people commit more crimes."[7] FBI Director James Comey also commented on the trend. He warned of a "chill wind blowing through American law enforcement" that may make "officers reluctant to get out of their cars and do the work that controls violent crime."[8]

Johnson was not affiliated with the Black Lives Matter movement. However, many people associated his actions with the movement. David Clark, a black sheriff in Milwaukee, Wisconsin, remarked, "the violence- and hate-filled messages pouring out of Black Lives Matter seek exactly this kind of bloody resolution, or revolution, though they cannot admit it in polite society."[9]

Many people in the Black Lives Matter movement reacted to the Dallas shootings with dismay. They did not want the movement to lose strength because of the shooter's actions. They also mourned the deaths of the slain police. Sir Maejor, a Black Lives Matter organizer, expressed his conflicting emotions about the shooting: "I understand

PRESIDENT OBAMA WEIGHS IN

In the wake of the Dallas police deaths, President Barack Obama urged Americans not to ignore the Black Lives Matter protests. People "cannot simply turn away and dismiss those in peaceful protest as troublemakers or paranoid," he said.[10] The president reminded Americans that racism still affects many and that the country still needs to improve race relations.

However, Obama also cautioned against sweeping generalizations about police and racial bias. He warned activists not to forget that "the vast majority of police officers are doing a really good job and are trying to protect people and do so fairly and without racial bias."[11]

why it was done," he said. "I don't encourage it, I don't condone it, I don't justify it. But I understand it." The Black Lives Matter movement reminded the media, "Black activists have raised the call for an end to violence, not an escalation of it." Maejor emphasized this point, saying, "Black Lives Matter doesn't condone shooting law enforcement."[12]

The Dallas police chief, who is black, responded to the police shootings and protests in an unexpected way. He encouraged protesters to join the police force. "We're hiring," he said. "We'll put you in your neighborhood, and we will help you resolve some of the problems you're protesting about."[13]

Dr. Brian Williams is a black surgeon in Dallas who helped care for several of the wounded police officers. At a press conference updating the public on his patients, he explained how complicated the situation was for him. He discussed his allegiance toward law enforcement. But he also expressed fears for the safety of black men at the hands of the police. "I want Dallas police also to see me, a black man, and understand that I support you, I will defend you and I will care for you," he said. "That doesn't mean that I do not fear you."[14]

FOUR
BLOODY DAYS

Over the course of four summer days in 2016, violence perpetrated by and against the police was a daily occurrence. The story of these bloody days captures the complex nature of the discussion about race, the police, and force.

JULY 5, 2016

Police in Baton Rouge, Louisiana, responded to a call saying a man outside a convenience store had a gun. Two white police officers shot and killed the suspect, Alton Sterling. After the shooting, the police retrieved a gun from Sterling's pocket. A bystander filmed the shooting and then shared the video on the Internet.

JULY 6, 2016

A police officer shot and killed Philando Castile, an African American man, after pulling him over during a traffic stop in Falcon Heights, Minnesota. Castile's girlfriend filmed his last breaths and broadcast the scene live on Facebook.

Diamond Reynolds, the girlfriend of Philando Castile, attends a protest outside the Minnesota governor's residence.

JULY 8, 2016

Dallas police killed Micah Johnson with a bomb.

A Black Lives Matter protester refuses to leave the street during a demonstration in Baton Rouge.

THE FUTURE OF BLACK LIVES MATTER

The Black Lives Matter movement is evolving to meet the needs of black people and respond to individual incidents of police racial bias. The movement has set forth many specific goals that it hopes will reduce police violence, including requiring quick legal investigations into police shootings of black people. The movement is also focusing on a wide variety of issues affecting African Americans, such as the way poor education contributes to high crime.

The manner in which people express support for Black Lives Matter is also evolving. Tennis star Serena Williams raised her fist in allegiance to the movement at the famous

Wimbledon tournament. Football player Colin Kaepernick started a wave of athletes who kneeled during the national anthem to show their support for Black Lives Matter.

The movement's narrative is likely to change as American police change. But activists hope that as the country grows, Black Lives Matter will shift its focus to new areas in which black lives can be improved.

SAY HER NAME

Black women who have experienced negative or even deadly interactions with law enforcement often do not get the attention that black men do. The organizers behind the Say Her Name movement hope to bring attention to police violence against black women. Launched in 2015, the movement highlights dozens of stories in which police harmed or killed black girls and women.

The first story in the report is about Eleanor Bumpurs. She was a woman in her sixties who was behind on rent. When police arrived at her apartment to evict her, she refused to open the door. The police then broke into her apartment. After Bumpurs threatened the officers with a kitchen knife, police shot her twice. Bumpurs died from her wounds.

| DISCUSSION STARTERS |

• How do you think Black Lives Matter has encouraged people to talk about race?

• Why do you think All Lives Matter has been controversial?

THE FUTURE OF AMERICAN POLICING

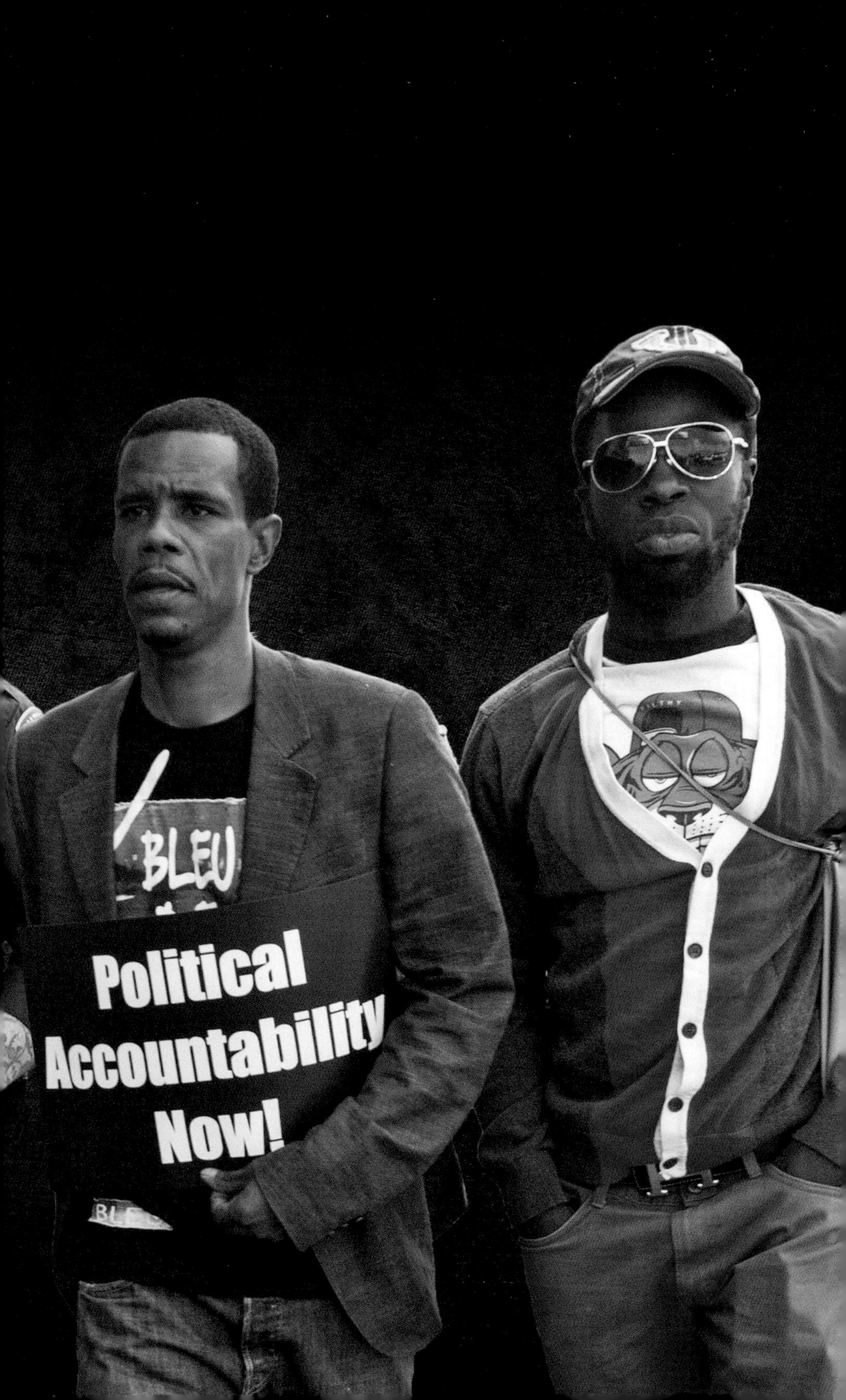
BLEU
Political
Accountability
Now!

The police exist to protect and serve their communities, but their history in the United States is tangled with incidents of racism and abuse. In recent years, several high-profile incidents involving racial violence have plagued police and citizens alike. Many politicians and community leaders are using these incidents to inspire a national conversation on how police and communities can have better relationships and how to heal racial discrimination.

Police forces across the country are working to implement improved policies, retrain officers, and reinforce community relationships. They hope to create a system in which police do not act out violently due to racial bias. Community leaders are also working to reshape the way the public perceives the police. They hope to rewrite the narrative of police as the enemy, and instead remind citizens that the police exist to promote safety.

COMMUNITY POLICING

Community policing is a philosophy in which civilians partner with the police to solve problems. One example of community policing is a neighborhood watch, in which civilians assist the police in identifying crime.

An officer speaks with a resident of the neighborhood he patrols.

When communities help the police do their job, both sides can learn to identify with one another. Other types of community policing allow law enforcement to help civilians in new ways. Police departments host safety lectures, participate in charity events, and assist at schools.

The fundamental principle behind community policing is that it is important for police officers to be upstanding and familiar members of their communities. When citizens recognize and feel comfortable with their police officers, they are more likely to find them trustworthy. When law enforcement builds relationships with the

MINORITY POLICE ASSOCIATIONS

People of color have a long history in police work. Though they have never represented the majority in American law enforcement, their numbers are growing. Different minority police groups exist to promote training and friendship and to bring attention to the specific problems facing their communities.

The National Black Police Association is a group with chapters across the United States. Its main goals are to improve the quality of life for black Americans, raise awareness of the importance of black police, and "be the conscience of the Criminal Justice System."[1]

The National Latino Peace Officers Association (NLPOA) is another key organization. The NLPOA's main goals are to improve professionalism and equality in the police force. One of the goals of the National Native American Law Enforcement Association is to facilitate cooperation between law enforcement officers and tribes. The Asian American Law Enforcement Association, headquartered in Chicago, also aims to promote good relationships between Asian Americans and the police.

community, officers can understand that the public relies on them for service and protection, not just enforcement and discipline.

DATA COLLECTION

In 2014, only two states required data to be collected after a police officer used deadly force. This contributed to the public perception that police were hiding or covering up some of their behavior. In 2015, several more states began requiring data to be collected each time a police officer used a gun or deadly force. Colorado, for example, now requires that every officer-involved shooting event must be reported to the Division of Criminal Justice. Officers must disclose the age, race, gender, and sexual orientation of themselves and the suspect. These records will help Colorado police departments determine whether bias is occurring.

Many states are also implementing new data collection standards for pedestrian stops and traffic stops. By recording details about the gender and ethnicity of the person stopped, police departments will learn how often their officers stop people of different races.

OFFICER RETRAINING

Police forces across the United States are working to improve and inspire their officers. The nation's largest force, the NYPD, is retraining all of its officers. Following the death of Eric Garner, the NYPD was harshly criticized for the way Officer Pantaleo behaved and also for the way the department responded. The new training aims to restore community trust in the NYPD and improve police behavior. It discourages verbal abuse and excessive force, teaches safe maneuvers for restraining suspects, and reminds officers that they are responsible for protecting and inspiring their community.

In the state of Washington, police officers are undergoing a new type of training meant to produce "guardians" rather than "warriors." The goal of this program is to train officers to communicate with and respect their communities. This training involves mediation and journaling, along with more traditional tactics such as simulations and lectures. Critics have said this "hug-a-thug" method of training does not prepare officers for the difficult and dangerous world of street policing.[2] Still, supporters of the new training program hope it will improve community-police relationships.

A RENEWED FOCUS ON THE COMMUNITY

Many observers have responded to police shootings by asserting that communities are just as much to blame for the violence as the police. They suggest fewer police killings would occur if community members were not acting recklessly.

The city of Chicago has struggled with gun violence. During one weekend in August 2016, 65 people in the city were shot, and 13 of those victims died.[3] The majority of these gun deaths were in black neighborhoods. Some experts believe cities such as Chicago need to focus more on gun laws, community reform, poverty, and education. They feel these issues are more problematic than police violence.

In 2014, a white police officer in Chicago killed a 17-year-old African American, Laquan McDonald, by shooting him 16 times. At the time of his death, McDonald was holding a small knife. Video of the incident ignited public outrage.

McDonald lived in a poor, high-crime neighborhood. He had been raised by a combination of family members and foster care. At one point, he admitted to a state worker that he had sold drugs, been involved with a gang, and been shot at. He had been suspended and expelled from school, been arrested, and served time in juvenile detention centers. The rough community in which he grew up had affected his life negatively.

THE MOBILE JUSTICE APP

One of the problems with smartphone video footage is that it can be deleted. The Mobile Justice app was created to ensure that any video of a police interaction could be instantly saved in its system. A user simply uses the app to film an incident. As soon as he or she stops recording, the video is automatically sent to the local American Civil Liberties Union office.

Chicago mayor Rahm Emanuel tried to use the public's anger at the incident as a way to inspire positive change. "I believe this is a moment that can build bridges of understanding rather than become a barrier of misunderstanding," he said.[4]

Emanuel was not alone in trying to draw attention to both sides of the debate. Many have responded to incidents such as McDonald's death by pointing to the high crime rates that affect cities across the nation. Many analysts believe crime in the community is a larger threat than police violence. One black Chicago officer lamented the public outrage at recent police shootings. "There are things to protest, but you attack us instead of attacking the actions of the gangbangers that you know, the people that you know have the guns," he said.[5] The officer's comments reflect the feelings of many Americans. They believe the anger directed at the police should be turned instead toward individuals committing crimes.

RATE A COP

In 2016, software developers created an app called Excuse Me Officer, which allows users to quickly report their observations about a police officer. Users are encouraged to rate officer interactions that were good as well as bad. The makers of the app hope it will "praise the good cops and expose the bad."[6]

MENTAL HEALTH

In the wake of recent officer-involved shootings, some observers have wondered whether better mental health screening of officers could reduce the frequency of these incidents. This idea is not new. In 1967, a governmental commission recommended that anyone who wanted to become a police officer should take a personality test. This test would screen recruits to be sure they were the right fit for police work. Most police departments ignored this recommendation until 1991, when the Rodney King beating caused a surge of public anger toward the police.

Today, approximately 90 percent of police departments screen applicants using a psychological test.[7] This is typically made up of a written test and an interview with a psychologist. The test determines whether applicants have the right personality to be police officers or whether they show signs of not being able to handle the stresses of the job.

Approximately 5 percent of police recruits do not pass their psychological exam, which means they are not allowed to become police officers. Law enforcement officials and civilians alike are calling for better mental health screening and care for police. They hope that identifying underlying mental health problems may prevent incidents of police killings. For example, approximately 15 to 18 percent of police are estimated to suffer from post-traumatic stress disorder (PTSD).[8] This disorder can affect people in different ways, but a common outcome is violent behavior. Mental health experts believe improving PTSD treatment for officers could drastically reduce police brutality.

Other observers are encouraging police departments to require all officers to submit to racial bias testing. These exams would reveal the extent to which an officer's racial bias affects the way he or she works. Then, depending on the results of the test, the police department could retrain, reassign, or even dismiss the officer.

NEW TECHNOLOGIES

The same technologies that bring police violence into the spotlight can also help improve community-police relationships. Smartphones captured the deaths of Eric Garner, Philando Castile, Alton Sterling, and many others. Footage of these incidents sparked anger in those who felt the police had acted inappropriately. It also enraged those who felt the police were being unfairly criticized.

As of 2015, approximately 72 percent of American adults owned smartphones.[9] As a result, a large majority of people can record their own interactions with police and record police interactions with others. This ability makes many people feel more comfortable. They believe an officer is less likely to act inappropriately if his or her actions are being recorded. Civilians can also use their

Body cams can help give the public a better understanding of the events that occur during interactions with police.

videos as evidence in cases of police misbehavior. Some officers find this type of video surveillance intrusive or distracting. Others welcome it, saying the video will accurately record their behavior.

Law enforcement has also embraced video recording. Most police cars have video cameras mounted on their dashboards. Although these cameras record the interactions officers have in front of their cars, they cannot record every detail. To solve this problem, approximately 95 percent of police departments in the United States hope to eventually use small cameras mounted on officers' bodies.[10] These body cams will be better at capturing the

KEEPING TRACK

Historically, no laws existed requiring law enforcement to report the number of arrest-related deaths. These are classified as deaths occurring at any point between a police interview, an arrest, and a suspect's arrival at the jail. Some private organizations have kept their own tallies, but these are not always accurate. Without a full understanding of the number of arrest-related deaths each year, it is difficult to find effective ways to solve the problem.

When the Death in Custody Reporting Act became law in 2014, many were hopeful this problem would change. The law required police departments to provide details about arrest-related deaths each quarter. However, few departments complied.

dialogue and interactions between officers and civilians. They will also be better at recording the things officers see. For example, if a suspect reaches toward his or her pocket suddenly, this action could be missed on a dash cam but recorded on a body cam. This additional evidence could help police officers explain their reactions.

Most observers do not believe new technologies are the ultimate solution to the problems between police and community members—nor do they believe technology can prevent racial discrimination. However, many hope these new tools can provide valuable data about the way people interact with the police.

A WORK IN PROGRESS

Police have weathered many storms throughout the history of the United States. Officers have overcome conflict, witnessed atrocities, and protected those who needed their help. But some have also participated in racial discrimination, both through individual actions and by enforcing racist laws.

Americans are learning more about the role racial bias plays in everyday interactions. By encouraging people to have conversations about race, racial bias, and the police, many observers hope American police departments will not only heal but also grow stronger.

| DISCUSSION STARTERS |

- Witnesses often record police interactions. How do you think the actions of a witness can influence the way a police officer behaves?

- How do you think a police officer's mental health affects the way he or she behaves?

- How have the police adapted to improve their relationships with the people they serve?

ESSENTIAL FACTS

SIGNIFICANT EVENTS

- On March 3, 1991, Rodney King was beaten during an arrest by white police officers in Los Angeles, California. Footage of the beating caused a national uproar. In 1992, after the officers were found not guilty, Los Angeles erupted in riots.

- On July 17, 2014, Eric Garner was killed during a police encounter when Officer Daniel Pantaleo used an illegal choke hold to subdue him. Footage of Garner's arrest quickly went viral.

- On July 7, 2016, Micah Johnson fired on a group of white police officers supervising a protest over recent police killings of unarmed black men. Johnson killed five officers and injured an additional seven.

KEY PLAYERS

- In the late 1960s, Illinois governor Otto Kerner chaired an investigation into the causes of racial violence. The Kerner Commission detailed many systemic problems in American culture, including unequal job opportunities, poor housing, and insufficient education for African Americans.

- In the 1980s, President Ronald Reagan and his wife, Nancy, made the fight against drugs a top priority. Racial and ethnic minorities were disproportionately arrested for drug-related crimes.

- Alton Sterling, Philando Castile, Freddie Gray, and Michael Brown were among a number of black men who were killed in police altercations between 2014 and 2016.

IMPACT ON SOCIETY

The conversation about race, racism, and American law enforcement is constantly evolving. Police departments are working to improve their forces, prevent incidents of excessive force, and strengthen the bonds they share with their communities. Civilian groups, such as Black Lives Matter, are encouraging communities to interact peacefully with the police, respect law enforcement, and behave kindly to others. Both police and civilians are taking steps to mend this tense relationship. As incidents occur in the future, both sides will focus on maintaining an open, respectful dialogue.

QUOTE

"We can and must do better to institute the best practices that reduce the appearance or reality of racial bias in law enforcement."

—*President Barack Obama*

GLOSSARY

ACQUITTAL
The act of setting free by declaring not guilty.

ADRENALINE
A hormone the body produces during times of stress.

BIAS
Prejudice in favor of or against one thing, person, or group compared with another, usually in a way considered to be unfair.

CIVIL COURT
A court dealing with disagreements between individuals or groups. Cases in civil court typically have monetary fines as punishment for the guilty party.

DISCRIMINATION
Unfair treatment of other people, usually because of race, age, or gender.

INDICT
To formally accuse someone of a crime.

INTEGRATE
To make schools, parks, and other facilities available to people of all races on an equal basis.

MARGINALIZATION

The act of placing someone in a marginal, or lower, level of importance.

MISCONDUCT

Improper or unlawful behavior.

POST-TRAUMATIC STRESS DISORDER

A mental health condition brought on by a traumatic event and is usually characterized by irritability, anxiety, depression, and insomnia.

PROSECUTE

To pursue a criminal conviction.

PROTOCOL

A set of routine behaviors, practices, or rules.

SEGREGATE

To separate groups of people based on race, gender, ethnicity, or other factors.

TASER

A weapon police use to electronically stun suspects.

UNCONSTITUTIONAL

Being inconsistent with the constitution of a state or society.

ADDITIONAL RESOURCES

SELECTED BIBLIOGRAPHY

Farbota, Kim. "Black Crime Rates: What Happens When Numbers Aren't Neutral." *Huffington Post*. Huffington Post, 2 Sept. 2015. Web. 15 Oct. 2016.

Gates, Henry Louis, Jr., and Kevin M. Burke. *And Still I Rise: Black America since MLK*. New York: Ecco, 2015. Print.

Geary, Daniel. "The Moynihan Report: An Annotated Edition." *Atlantic*. Atlantic Monthly Group, 14 Sept. 2015. Web. 16 Oct. 2016.

FURTHER READINGS

Edwards, Sue Bradford, and Duchess Harris. *Black Lives Matter*. Minneapolis: Abdo, 2016. Print.

Mullenbach, Cheryl. *Women in Blue: 16 Brave Officers, Forensics Experts, Police Chiefs, and More*. Chicago: Chicago Review, 2016. Print.

Rissman, Rebecca. *Rodney King and the L.A. Riots*. Minneapolis: Abdo, 2014. Print.

WEBSITES

To learn more about Race in America, visit **abdobooklinks.com**. These links are routinely monitored and updated to provide the most current information available.

FOR MORE INFORMATION

For more information on this subject, contact or visit the following organizations:

AMERICAN POLICE HALL OF FAME & MUSEUM
6350 Horizon Drive
Titusville, FL 32780
321-264-0911
http://www.aphf.org/

Visit this museum to learn about the history and current trends of American law enforcement. Interactive displays, simulators, and more than 11,000 historical artifacts make this museum a fascinating visit.

BLACK POLICE PRECINCT AND COURTHOUSE MUSEUM
480 NW 11th Street
Miami, FL 33136
305-329-2513
http://historicalblackprecinct.org/

Visit this museum to learn about the African American police officers who worked in the 1940s, 1950s, and 1960s in this Florida precinct.

THE NEW YORK CITY POLICE MUSEUM
45 Wall Street
New York, NY 10005
212-480-3100
https://www.nycpm.org/

This museum is dedicated to preserving the history and telling the stories of the nation's largest and most famous police department. The exhibitions and collections highlight the way the NYPD has grown to accommodate a changing city.

SOURCE
NOTES

CHAPTER 1. "I CAN'T BREATHE"

1. Al Baker, J. David Goodman, and Benjamin Mueller. "Beyond the Chokehold: The Path to Eric Garner's Death." *New York Times*. New York Times, 13 June 2015. Web. 9 Feb. 2017.

2. Ibid.

3. Ibid.

4. Ibid.

5. Matt Sledge and Saki Knafo. "NYPD 'Emasculated' Its Own Chokehold Ban, Watchdog Agency Finds." *Huffington Post*. Huffington Post, 8 Oct. 2014. Web. 9 Feb. 2017.

CHAPTER 2. A HISTORY OF SEPARATION AND SEGREGATION

1. "Slavery in America." *History*. A&E Television Networks, n.d. Web. 9 Feb. 2017.

2. "The Founders' Constitution." *University of Chicago*. University of Chicago, 2000. Web. 9 Feb. 2017.

3. "Top 5 Questions About the KKK." *PBS*. WGBH Educational Foundation, n.d. Web. 9 Feb. 2017.

4. "Slavery in America." *History*. A&E Television Networks, n.d. Web. 9 Feb. 2017.

5. "Black Legislators: Primary Sources." *PBS*. PBS Online/WGBH, n.d. Web. 9 Feb. 2017.

6. "Japanese-American Relocation." *History*. A&E Television Networks, n.d. Web. 9 Feb. 2017.

CHAPTER 3. POLICE AND THE FIGHT FOR EQUAL RIGHTS

1. "'Our Nation Is Moving toward Two Societies, One Black, One White—Separate and Unequal': Excerpts from the Kerner Report." *History Matters*. American Social History Productions, n.d. Web. 9 Feb. 2017.

2. Martha Biondi. *To Stand and Fight: The Struggle for Civil Rights in Postwar New York City*. Cambridge, MA: Harvard UP, 2003. Print. 230.

3. Emily Badger. "How Section 8 Became a 'Racial Slur.'" *Washington Post*. Washington Post, 15 June 2015. Web. 9 Feb. 2017.

4. Jamie Fellner. "Race, Drugs, and Law Enforcement in the United States." *Human Rights Watch*. Human Rights Watch, 19 June 2009. Web. 9 Feb. 2017.

5. "Poverty in the United States: Frequently Asked Questions." *National Poverty Center*. University of Michigan, n.d. Web. 9 Feb. 2017.

6. "Poverty." *The State of Working America*. Economic Policy Institute, n.d. Web. 9 Feb. 2017.

CHAPTER 4. TO SERVE AND PROTECT

1. "Training/Academy Life." *Discover Policing*. Discover Policing, n.d. Web. 9 Feb. 2017.

2. Ibid.

3. "Tennessee v. Garner." *FindLaw*. FindLaw, n.d. Web. 9 Feb. 2017.

4. Chase Madar. "Why It's Impossible to Indict a Cop." *Nation*. Nation, 25 Nov. 2014. Web. 9 Feb. 2017.

5. Zak Cheney Rice. "Michigan Judge Pulls No Punches in 30-Minute Sentencing Tirade against Police Officer." *Mic*. Mic Network, 3 Feb. 2016. Web. 9 Feb. 2017.

6. Jaxon Van Derbeken. "Bigoted Texts 'Disgraced' SFPD, Chief Says, Vowing Rapid Action." *San Francisco Gate*. Hearst Communications, 16 Mar. 2015. Web. 9 Feb. 2017.

7. Ibid.

8. Sasha Goldstein. "Four San Francisco Police Officers Investigated for Racist, Homophobic Text Messages Sent to Ex-Cop Convicted of Corruption." *New York Daily News*. NYDailyNews.com, 16 Mar. 2015. Web. 9 Feb. 2017.

9. Chase Madar. "Why It's Impossible to Indict a Cop." *Nation*. Nation, 25 Nov. 2014. Web. 9 Feb. 2017.

10. "Diversity in Law Enforcement: A Literature Review." *US Department of Justice*. US Department of Justice, Jan. 2015. Web. 9 Feb. 2017.

11. Jeremy Ashkenas and Haeyoun Park. "The Race Gap in America's Police Departments." *New York Times*. New York Times, 8 Apr. 2015. Web. 9 Feb. 2017.

12. Carl Bialik. "Police Killings Almost Never Lead to Murder Charges." *FiveThirtyEight*. FiveThirtyEight, 1 May 2015. Web. 9 Feb. 2017.

13. Matt Ferner and Nick Wing. "Here's How Many Cops Got Convicted of Murder Last Year for On-Duty Shootings." *Huffington Post*. Huffington Post, 13 Jan. 2016. Web. 9 Feb. 2017.

14. Alex Q. Arbuckle. "May 13, 1985: The Bombing of MOVE." *Mashable*. Mashable, n.d. Web. 9 Feb. 2017.

15. Alan Yuhas. "Philadelphia's Osage Avenue Police Bombing, 30 Years On: 'This Story Is a Parable.'" *Guardian*. Guardian News and Media, 13 May 2015. Web. 9 Feb. 2017.

16. Rick Noack. "5 Countries Where Most Police Officers Do Not Carry Firearms—And It Works Well." *Washington Post*. Washington Post, 8 July 2016. Web. 9 Feb. 2017.

17. Carrie Dann. "Eric Holder: 'It's the Right Time for Me to Go.'" *NBC News*. NBC News, 26 Sept. 2014. Web. 9 Feb. 2017.

CHAPTER 5. WALKING WHILE BLACK

1. Joseph Goldstein. "Judge Rejects New York's Stop-and-Frisk Policy." *New York Times*. New York Times, 12 Aug. 2013. Web. 9 Feb. 2017.

2. "Obama Says Nation Must Take Steps to Address Racial Bias in Policing." *Newsmax*. Thomson/Reuters, 7 July 2016. Web. 9 Feb. 2017.

3. Quoctrung Bui and Amanda Cox. "Surprising New Evidence Shows Bias in Police Use of Force but Not in Shootings." *New York Times*. New York Times, 11 July 2016. Web. 9 Feb. 2017.

4. "O'Reilly: America Is Not a Racist Nation, as the Far Left Claims." *FOX News*. FOX News Network, 24 June 2015. Web. 9 Feb. 2017.

5. Danielle Paquette. "Giuliani: 'White Police Officers Wouldn't Be There If You Weren't Killing Each Other.'" *Washington Post*. Washington Post, 23 Nov. 2014. Web. 9 Feb. 2017.

6. Sharon LaFraniere and Andrew W. Lehren. "The Disproportionate Risks of Driving While Black." *New York Times*. New York Times, 24 Oct. 2015. Web. 9 Feb. 2017.

7. "President Obama Says US 'Not Even Close' to Resolving Police-Community Tensions." *Fortune*. Time, 14 July 2016. Web. 9 Feb. 2017.

8. "Top Moments from the Vice Presidential Debate between Mike Pence and Tim Kaine." *Vice News*. Vice News, 4 Oct. 2016. Web. 9 Feb. 2017.

9. Ibid.

10. S. A. Miller. "Donald Trump: Black Americans 'Not Necessarily Wrong' about Police Abuses." *Washington Times*. Washington Times, 12 July 2016. Web. 9 Feb. 2017.

CHAPTER 6. THE ROLE OF FEAR

1. Jeffrey M. Jones. "In US, Confidence in Police Lowest in 22 Years." *Gallup*. Gallup, 19 June 2015. Web. 9 Feb. 2017.

2. "Cops Surround Sikh Man in US as Callers Report 'Muslim with Sword.'" *Tribune*. Tribune Trust, 22 Sept. 2016. Web. 9 Feb. 2017.

3. Jon Schuppe. "Jon Burge Case: Police Torture Scandal Still Casts Long Shadow over Chicago." *NBC News*. NBC News, 16 Aug. 2015. Web. 9 Feb. 2017.

4. "Police Officer Fired after Racist Selfie Emerges." *NBC4i.com*. Nexstar Broadcasting, 29 Sept. 2016. Web. 9 Feb. 2017.

5. Shane Shifflett, et al. "Police Abuse Complaints by Black Chicagoans Dismissed Nearly 99 Percent of the Time." *Huffington Post*. Huffington Post, 7 Dec. 2015. Web. 9 Feb. 2017.

6. Joseph P. Williams. "When It Comes to Police Brutality, Fear Is Also a Factor." *US News and World Report*. US News and World Report, 5 Dec. 2014. Web. 9 Feb. 2017.

7. Ibid.

8. Ibid.

9. Kareem Abdul-Jabbar. "There Is Terror on Both Sides of the Badge." *Time*. Time, 13 July 2016. Web. 9 Feb. 2017.

10. Kareem Abdul-Jabbar. "The Coming Race War Won't Be about Race." *Time*. Time, 17 Aug. 2014. Web. 9 Feb. 2017.

CHAPTER 7. BLACK LIVES MATTER

1. Megan Lasher. "Read the Full Transcript of Jesse Williams' Powerful Speech on Race at the BET Awards." *Time*. Time, 27 June 2016. Web. 9 Feb. 2017.

2. Karen Mizoguchi. "Jesse Williams Speaks Out about Petition to Get Him Fired from *Grey's Anatomy*: 'Not a Single Sane Sentence in Their Claim.'" *People*. Time, 6 July 2016. Web. 9 Feb. 2017.

3. German Lopez. "Why You Should Stop Saying 'All Lives Matter,' Explained in 9 Different Ways." *Vox*. Vox Media, 11 July 2016. Web. 9 Feb. 2017.

4. Tamara Keith and Amita Kelly. "Hillary Clinton's 3-Word Misstep: 'All Lives Matter.'" *NPR*. NPR, 24 June 2015. Web. 9 Feb. 2017.

5. Jessica Chasmar. "Hillary Clinton Declares 'Black Lives Matter.'" *Washington Times*. Washington Times, 21 July 2015. Web. 9 Feb. 2017.

6. Steve Chapman. "Is This Rise in Crime a 'Ferguson Effect'?" *Chicago Tribune*. Chicago Tribune, 29 Jan. 2016. Web. 9 Feb. 2017.

7. Tim Hains. "O'Reilly: How "Black Lives Matter" Is Causing Increased Crime, Murder." *RealClearPolitics*. RealClearPolitics.com, 25 May 2016. Web. 9 Feb. 2017.

8. Steve Chapman. "Is This Rise in Crime a 'Ferguson Effect'?" *Chicago Tribune*. Chicago Tribune, 29 Jan. 2016. Web. 9 Feb. 2017.

9. Valerie Richardson. "Dallas Police Chief Invites Black Lives Matter Protesters to Join Department." *Washington Times*. Washington Times, 11 July 2016. Web. 9 Feb. 2017.

10. Dave Boyer. "Obama Defends Black Lives Matter Protests at Police Memorial in Dallas." *Washington Times*. Washington Times, 12 July 2016. Web. 9 Feb. 2017.

11. Reena Flores. "Obama Defends Black Lives Matter Movement as Protests Heat Up." *CBS News*. CBS Interactive, 10 July 2016. Web. 9 Feb. 2017.

12. "Black Lives Matter Condemns Dallas, Pushes Forward with Protests." *CBS News*. CBS Interactive, 8 July 2016. Web. 9 Feb. 2017.

13. Valerie Richardson. "Dallas Police Chief Invites Black Lives Matter Protesters to Join Department." *Washington Times*. Washington Times, 11 July 2016. Web. 9 Feb. 2017.

14. Seema Yasmin. "Black Doctor Who Treated Dallas Shooting Victims Speaks Honestly about Supporting and Fearing Police." *Dallas News*. Dallas Morning News, 11 July 2016. Web. 9 Feb. 2017.

CHAPTER 8. THE FUTURE OF AMERICAN POLICING

1. "About Us." *National Black Police Association*. National Black Police Association, n.d. Web. 9 Feb. 2017.

2. Kimberly Kindy. "Creating Guardians, Calming Warriors." *Washington Post*. Washington Post, 10 Dec. 2015. Web. 9 Feb. 2017.

3. "Chicago's Alarming Gun Violence." *CBS News*. CBS Interactive, n.d. Web. 9 Feb. 2017.

4. "Dash-Cam Video Released Showing Laquan McDonald's Fatal Shooting." *NBC Chicago*. NBCUniversal Media, 17 Dec. 2015. Web. 9 Feb. 2017.

5. William Lee. "For African-American Police Officers, a Foot in Two Worlds." *Chicago Tribune*. Chicago Tribune, 10 Aug. 2016. Web. 9 Feb. 2017.

6. "About Us." *Excuse Me Officer*. Excuse Me Officer, n.d. Web. 18 Nov. 2016.

7. Timothy Roufa. "Psychological Exams and Screening for Police Officers." *The Balance*. About, 12 Oct. 2016. Web. 9 Feb. 2017.

8. Shaun King. "American Police, Who See Humanity at Its Worst, Must Be Regularly Tested and Treated for PTSD." *New York Daily News*. NYDailyNews. com, 9 Aug. 2016. Web. 9 Feb. 2017.

9. Jacob Poushter. "Smartphone Ownership and Internet Usage Continues to Climb in Emerging Economies." *Pew Research Center*. Pew Research Center, 22 Feb. 2016. Web. 9 Feb. 2017.

10. Mike Maciag. "Survey: Almost All Police Departments Plan to Use Body Cameras." *Governing*. e.Republic, 26 Jan. 2016. Web. 9 Feb. 2017.

INDEX

ABOUT THE AUTHORS

Duchess Harris is a professor and chair of the American Studies department at Macalester College. Her other secondary education publications are the coauthored books *Black Lives Matter* and *Hidden Human Computers: The Black Women of NASA* with Sue Bradford Edwards. Professor Harris earned a PhD in American Studies from the University of Minnesota. She was a postdoctoral fellow at the Institute on Race and Poverty at the University of Minnesota Law School. She received her Juris Doctorate from William Mitchell College of Law. In 2015, the Minnesota Association of Black Lawyers chose her to receive the Profiles in Courage Award. In 2016, Minnesota governor Mark Dayton appointed her to the Board of Public Defense.

Rebecca Rissman is an award-winning children's author. Her writing has been praised by *School Library Journal*, *Booklist*, *Creative Child Magazine*, and *Learning Magazine*. She has written more than 200 books about history, science, art, and culture. Rissman is especially interested in American history, with an emphasis on the military, the police, and the government. She has also written titles about slavery, the black power movement, and Rodney King and the Los Angeles riots. Rissman lives in Chicago, Illinois, with her husband and two daughters.